border terrier

understanding and caring for your dog

Written by
Kathy Wilkinson

border terrier

understanding and
caring for your dog

Written by
Kathy Wilkinson

Pet Book Publishing Company

The Old Hen House, St Martin's Farm, Zeals, Warminster, Wiltshire, BA12 6NZ.

Printed by Printworks Global Ltd. London/Hong Kong

ISBN: 978-1-906305-66-6
ISBN: 1-906305-66-8

Acknowledgements

The publishers would like to thank the following for help with photography: Colin Seddon, Bob and Carey Hand (Lutrabeck), Anara Hibberd (Biddestone), Jane Parker (Conundrum), Dawn Bladen (Emblehope), Jem and Helen Thomas (Daluce), and Ron and Kathy Wilkinson (Otterkin).

Contents

Introducing the Border Terrier

The Border Terrier is essentially a working terrier. He was bred to follow the horses when out with the hunt and be fit and able to go to ground to flush the fox at the end of the day.

Despite their working heritage, Border Terriers make good family pets and will get on well with children if mutual respect is established. However, no child should be left alone with a dog of any breed, as children do not always understand what upsets or worries a dog.

The Border is not designed to be a guard dog; he may bark at visitors then lick them once they are in the house! He loves to be with his owners; it would be sad for him to be left on his own in a kennel, especially if his owners are out at work all day and

then do not have the time for him in the evening. A bored dog soon becomes a destructive dog and, in the case of the Border, he may also become very vocal, which could cause problems with the neighbors.

This is one of the most adaptable of all breeds, and although he is naturally suited to country living, he can be content in an urban setting as long as he has sufficient exercise. He is, however, a great explorer, and will need a securely fenced garden, with no opportunity to dig himself out!

Most Borders have a tough exterior, but they can be sensitive, particularly if they are harshly treated. This is a dog that needs gentle handling and early socialization so that he becomes a model canine citizen.

Physical characteristics

The Border Terrier is a dog of small to medium size, built on racy lines, with an otter-like head, a short strong muzzle, a ribcage which should be able to be spanned by both hands, a level topline and a tail which is well set on, but not curled over the back.

He has a double coat, with an outer harsh topcoat to keep him relatively clean and dry and a soft undercoat to keep him warm. His topcoat will require handstripping about twice a year, which is something you can learn to do quite easily or employ a professional groomer, but ensure you ask that they handstrip him and not clip him. If his coat is clipped, the topcoat's protective layer is lost. Some books and websites incorrectly state this is a non-shedding breed, but nothing could be further from the truth; he requires twice yearly stripping to keep his coat short and help to reduce the amount of hairs shed.

There are four colors in the Breed Standard: red, wheaten, grizzle and tan and blue and tan – the latter two are the colors most seen today.

Exercising mind and body

The Border Terrier is a highly intelligent dog, bred
for an active life. He needs a variety of free running
exercise and lead walking to keep physically fit,
but he also needs to exercise his mind. A Border
Terrier needs to be trained in basic obedience and,
ideally, he should then be given a job to do. He can
compete in one of the canine sports, such as Agility
or Obedience, or you can channel his energies into
playing games and learning new tricks. It does not
matter what you do, as long as you understand that
providing mental stimulation is a vital part of caring
for this breed.

Understanding the Border

You should understand that your Border Terrier,
who runs off to chase rabbits and deer, and digs
frantically to unearth vermin, has a purpose which
encapsulates everything he is and does. He is a
terrier, with a strong prey drive, and hunting is the
name of the game.

He is not the breed for everyone, but if you love him
and care for him, train him as best you can without
losing your temper, forgive his misdemeanors as he
forgives yours, then you may have a friend for life.

He can get excited when you walk back in the room although you have only been gone two minutes, but he can also rip up a box of hankies and spread them over two rooms in that two minutes. If your Border has gone quiet and not come to find you after being left alone somewhere for a minute, he is definitely up to something!

If he has done something naughty, or made a mess, or gone to the toilet in the wrong place, all of that is your fault for not watching him properly, not his fault for just being who he is.

Living with animals

The Border Terrier is highly sociable and enjoys living in a pack, preferably with his own kind. However, he will mix with other breeds, especially if he has been socialized with other dogs from an early age.

A Border may be able to live with the family cat, particularly if you work at early interactions when your Border is a puppy. If, however, your cat is elderly or of a sensitive disposition, is it fair to disrupt its life? It would possibly be fatal to bring a kitten or an adult cat into a home where there is already a resident adult Border.

A Border might be trusted with small family pets such as rabbits and guinea pigs as much as I might be trusted in the same room as a bar of chocolate! The Border was bred to hunt and instinct can take over in a split second. Never take the risk of allowing your Border Terrier to be in the same room, or in the garden, with small animals, even if they appear to be securely caged.

Summing up

This is one of the most versatile and adaptable of all breeds – once smitten, there will be no other breed for you. However, take time to weigh up the pros and cons of this remarkable little dog, and go into ownership with your eyes wide open.

Right: *The Border is a true terrier at heart, with a strong hunting instinct.*

Tracing back
in time

If you have bought your Border Terrier as a companion, you may not think the breed's history is of much relevance to you. However, it is the key to understanding your Border Terrier's behavior, which is the result of years of breeding for particular traits.

The Border Terrier originated on the borders of England and Scotland. Most known texts refer to him being found on the border between Northumberland and Roxburghshire, although there were sightings and claims of Borders bred around the Lakeland area and Cumberland/Westmoreland counties.

Different areas of the borders had different strains of terriers and by hearsay, or some written texts from the 1800s, we learn there were Coquetdale Terriers and Rothbury Terriers, later known as the Bedlingtons, and Dandie Dinmonts. When people found a dog which was known for his working abilities, they could include his bloodline, and so the Border Terrier is probably an amalgamation of these different terrier types.

Working terriers were used to despatch vermin around the farm and they helped to control the fox population, which was a major hazard to sheep. These were fit, active dogs with the stamina and willingness to work all day – a trait that can be seen in present-day Border Terriers.

Borders were much prized as part of the entourage of the Foxhound packs and they enjoyed a long association with the Robson and Dodd families, who were masters of the pack in the 1800s through to the 1900s.

Their job was to follow horses over the rough terrain of the Northumberland and Roxburghshire hills and dales, and be ready to go to ground after a fox, bolting it if possible, and if it would not bolt, killing it. When it was still legal to hunt otter and badger, as well as fox, Border Terriers would assist with all those quarry, and masters of the hunt waxed eloquently about the working prowess of our breed.

Developing the breed

Border Terriers may have been exhibited in variety classes at dog shows as early as the 1870s in Newcastle upon Tyne and at agricultural shows around that time. The first show that scheduled the breed in a class of their own was the Bellingham show in 1881.

In 1913, the first Border Terrier was registered with the Kennel Club, but as the breed had not yet been recognized, it was registered under "Any Breed or Variety of British, Colonial or Foreign Dog – Not Classified". This was Miss M. Rew's Moss Trooper, a blue and tan dog sired by an unregistered dog called Sly out of Mr J. Robson's Chip, born on February 2nd 1912.

Between 1913 and 1919, only 41 Border Terriers were registered, but by the time of the inaugural meeting of the Border Terrier Club at Hawick in July 1920, over 150 registrations were made.

Breed recognition

At the first meeting at Hawick, some people were not happy about the breed seeking Kennel Club recognition. They felt it might ruin the breed and change it so it was not capable of doing the job for which it was originally intended.

However, breed enthusiasts drew up a Breed Standard, and in September 1920, the Kennel Club formally recognized the Border Terrier Club. Challenge Certificates were granted and within a matter of weeks they were awarded at the first Championship show.

The first Champion was made up in 1921. He was a dog called Teri, sired by North Tyne Gyp, a highly influential sire in those early days. The first female Champion was Liddesdale Bess, who was described by her owner, Mr Barton, as:

"a grand little bitch, short coupled, dark red with a short thickset coat with hair like wire, she stood on her legs like a thoroughbred horse and had feet like a cat".

In these early years, there were two Border Terriers that had a major impact on the breed's development. Rival and Revenge were owned by Adam Forester and nearly every Border Terrier in the modern era traced their lives back to one or both of those dogs.

The Border Terrier in the USA

The first Border Terrier was registered in the USA in 1927, although there may have been a few dogs imported from the UK before then. A trickle of dogs were imported during the 1930s, but more widespread recognition came in 1941 with the arrival of a bitch in whelp to the great Ch. Foxlair.

Below: Dedicated breeders worked hard to establish the Border Terrier on both sides of the Atlantic.

There were two enthusiasts who did much to develop the breed in its new home – William MacBain of the Diehard Border Terriers and Dr Merritt Pope with his Philibeg kennel. Appropriately they had the first male and female Champions in the breed: Am. Ch. Diehard Dandy and Am. Ch. Philibeg Red Miss.

Landmark wins for American Border Terriers include the first Terrier Group winner, Am. Ch. D. G. Wattie Irving of Dalquest, and Best in Show winner, Am. Ch. Workmore Waggoner.

The Border Terrier today

From small beginnings, the Border Terrier has grown in popularity. Initially this was fairly gradual, but in the last 20 years, it is true to say the breed has taken off. This is particularly the case in the UK and in Scandinavia, but it also has an enthusiastic following in the USA.

Fortunately the breed has retained the character and temperament that has made it so special, and it remains a hardy animal, built without exaggeration. It is imperative that breeders continue to strive for excellence and that the breed is passed on to future generations, remaining true to it original type and valued as a companion dog *par excellence*.

What should a Border Terrier look like?

The Breed Standard of the Border Terrier is essentially the same as the original one accepted by the Kennel Club in 1920. One amendment which was made quite quickly was a reduction in the recommended weight, with dogs going from 14-17 lb to 13-15½ lb, and bitches from not exceeding 15 lb to 11½-14 lb, guidelines which remain the same today.

Following its ongoing review of all Breed Standards in recent years, the Kennel Club in the UK has included a mandatory introductory paragraph to all Breed Standards, to ensure that judges of all breeds consider the ideal characteristics, temperament and

appearance of the breeds to ensure a dog is "fit for function" and that absolute soundness is essential, with breeders and judges urged at all times to be careful to avoid obvious conditions or exaggerations which would be detrimental in any way to the health, welfare or soundness of the breed.

General appearance

The description of the general appearance of the Border has to be one of the briefest among all Breed Standards – "Essentially a working terrier". Those who were initially against Kennel Club recognition of the breed, did not want the Border turned into "just another show dog", but wanted to make sure the breed would still be capable of doing a job. It was not just a preference that they might be able to work, it was "essential" that they could still work.

Characteristics and temperament

The Breed Standard asks that the dog should be able to follow a horse and combine activity with gameness. Good temperament is very important in any dog, but is a must in a dog that is your hunting partner.

Now that most Borders are companions and not workers, that essential make up of one who is a quiet companion when not working, and a devil underground when faced with a fox, is still essential

Points of anatomy

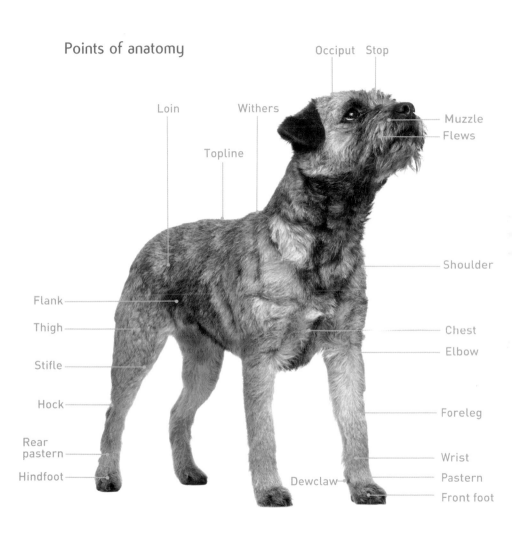

Occiput

Stop

Loin

Withers

Muzzle

Flews

Topline

Shoulder

Flank

Thigh

Chest

Stifle

Elbow

Hock

Foreleg

Rear
pastern

Wrist

Hindfoot

Dewclaw

Pastern

Front foot

and perhaps even more so. They should be a typical Jekyl and Hyde character, as soft and biddable as they come when on your knee but ready to tackle a fox if asked to do so.

Head and skull

Without the "head like that of an otter", the Border Terrier would not be a distinctive breed. People in the breed argue over how otter-like the head should be.

Personally, I believe it refers to the flow-through from the nose to the top of the skull and the flatness of the skull. The Border should not have a distinct "stop" at the top of his nose, neither should he have a prominent top of skull, but it should be level.

If you take your hand, palm down, thumb on one side of the Border's head and fingers on the other, just in front of the ears and look at the head from the side, the resemblance to an otter in a good example of the breed is more obvious. The Border should be "moderately" broad in skull, not with a skull so wide that it resembles a teddy bear!

The Border's muzzle should be short and strong, neither long nor weak and snipey. A strong muzzle will usually contain large teeth, both attributes helpful in a working dog which, if he cannot bolt his fox, may be required to despatch or hold him.

Eyes

The eyes are dark with a keen expression. Light eyes look foreign and spoil the desired keen expression.

No size or shape is mentioned, but we may assume that a large, protruding eye would not give the correct keen expression and might be a danger to the dog when tackling a fox, being easily damaged.

Nose

A black nose is preferable, but a liver or flesh colored nose is not a serious fault. Some dogs lose a little nose colouration in the winter and regain their black nose in the summer, known by the most technical term of 'winter nose'. There are more serious aspects of failure for a working terrier than a flesh colored nose.

Throughout the Standard, we can see that major faults are those that would affect the dog's ability to work.

Ears

Ears should be small, v shaped, of "moderate" thickness and dropping forward close to the cheek. Relating everything to a dog's ability to work, large ears, while unattractive, may also be prone to damage in a confrontation with a fox.

Very thick ears may not lie close to the cheek and so, may render the dog susceptible to a bite, as might ears which are prominent above the level of the skull. So small, v shaped ears, lying close to the side of the head have become the type we see in most show and working Borders today. Large 'houndy' ears neither look the part, nor do they help with the achievement of a "keen expression".

Mouth

A scissor bite is required, with top teeth closely overlapping the bottom teeth and no significant gap between the rows of teeth, either on top (overshot) or from the bottom (undershot).

It is important that a dog or bitch to be bred from has a good scissor bite, as undershot or overshot mouths are highly undesirable. They are hereditary and therefore may be passed to future generations.

Neck

The neck is "of moderate length". A short neck sometimes indicates the dog is upright in shoulder and, in any event, does not give the right look to the whole dog. It is sometimes accompanied by a body which is too chunky and short. The ideal is a moderate neck, which while giving an appearance of elegance, should not be swan-like.

Forequarters

While the Standard states "Forelegs straight, not too heavy in bone." most judges would, I think, agree that along with straight front legs, a Border should not be wide in front, nor so narrow that it looks like both legs are coming out of the same hole!

Going back to the requirement for a Border to be

able to follow a horse, a Border which is wide in front is not going to be able to keep up the long easy strides needed at a gallop.

"Not too heavy in bone" is also important, as a dog with heavy bone in his front legs, will normally have a wide ribcage and be too heavy for his function in life.

Body

The description of the body of a Border gives more information than most parts of the Standard, which is understandable when he needs the correct shape and length to do his job. The first part of the body description is broken into three parts: *"Deep, narrow, fairly long."*

Lets deal with those as separate items, although a dog should not be an amalgamation of distinctly separate things, but all parts should fit together to combine in style and essence into one being.

"Deep"

A dog with insufficient substance will sometimes not be deep in body. There is no further indication in the standard as to how deep the body should go; it will be a matter for judges to debate, although if everything is in moderation, stopping some way short of its paws may be a good thing!

"Narrow"

This is one of the most important words in the Standard. A dog which is not narrow cannot follow a very narrow fox into its earth, or he may get down into the earth and be unable to turn and get back out again, or be unable to manoeuvre himself out of a tight spot. Form follows function most definitely in this part of the Standard, which is more descriptive than in most other places, giving an indication of the importance ascribed to it by people working their dogs.

"Fairly long"

One of the dictionary definitions of "fairly" is "moderately"! So no – the terrier men of old did not move far from their "moderate" wording and we should remember that here as well.

The ribs of the Border Terrier should be "carried well back, but not over-sprung, as a terrier should be capable of being spanned by both hands behind the shoulder."

A judge demonstrates he knows nothing about the breed if he doesn't attempt to span the dogs on the table. A good judge of the breed will also check where the ribcage ends. A short, cobby dog which is chunky and of heavy bone, will often have a short ribcage to match his chunky legs and thickset, short neck, poor thing!

Generally, a dog with a moderate length of body and the correct ribcage, length and width, will be flexible and move well. This will be aided by strong loins, which concludes the description of the Border's body.

Hindquarters

The Border Terrier is required by the Standard to have "racy" hindquarters. I would describe this as having a "waist" after the end rib. While he should be well covered and healthy, he should look like an

Power comes from the hindquarters.

athlete rather than a couch potato. It does not mean that he should be weak in the hindquarters.

There is no mention in the standard of not wanting cow hocks, or legs which rub together when the dog walks along, which some dogs do. However, I would expect a judge to penalise these faults.

Stifles should be moderately bent. The correct bend of stifle enables the dog to push off from his hindquarters, moving efficiently and effectively at whatever speed he is employing, be it trot, canter or gallop!

Feet

A dog which is required to follow the horses should have small feet with thick pads. Like a horse, any injury to the foot will impact on the ability to do the job and the smaller the foot, the less likely it is to be injured. As the Border has to run on harsh terrain all day, this is very important and many a judge can be seen lifting the dog's foot to check on the thickness of the pads.

Those 'in the know' describe the size of the feet as "cat-like". Long hare-like feet are not wanted and the dog's foot should be upright and not down at the pasterns. Again, form follows function and a dog with a good set of feet will be able to do the job.

Tail

The tail should be moderately short; fairly thick at the base and then tapering. It is set on high, carried gaily, but not curled over the back. In a dog of moderate length, the tail, being an extension of the spine, will match. A tail that is thick at the base and tapers is referred to as 'carrot shaped'.

The tail is carrot-shaped and is set on high.

There is a ring of light hairs about one-third of the way up the Border's tail. This covers a scent gland and is not any cause for concern. All Borders have it, some being more noticeable than others.

The tail should come straight off the top of the back and when a dog is being shown, the ideal place for the tail is at 10 to the hour, or 10 past the hour depending on which way you are looking at your dog. If your dog's head in on the right-hand side as you look at him, his tail should be at about 10 to the hour.

The position of the tail when the dog is in repose is different – many a bored Border will have his tail down, but show him something interesting, or take him for a walk, and his tail will be up!

Movement

Judges place a lot of emphasis on movement and this is the right thing to do, as a dog which moves well with efficiency is more likely to be able to run with the horses all day and not be so tired that he cannot go to ground.

The Standard is again quite short on requirements in this section, asking only for "the soundness to follow a horse", though it could be argued that it requires steady, true, efficient ground covering movement for a working dog to keep up with the horses.

Dogs which flip front legs, or fail to drive from the rear are going to be more easily tired and incapable of keeping up. So we must pick up on the word "soundness" and expand on it.

As a judge, I find it hard to forgive the flipping front paws or cow hocks, the elbows which flap around in the breeze and the high goose stepping which indicates straight shoulders.

Soundness and true straight forward movement, which propels the dog easily across the show ring and across the hunting field, is a joy to witness.

As the dog walks towards the judge, you should not see any flipping or flapping. Going away from you, you should see no cow hocks and viewed from the side, propulsion from the rear can be more readily appreciated.

Some handlers in other breeds string their dogs up so the front feet are nearly off the ground when walking. Borders should be moved nicely on a loose lead, so the dog's true movement cannot be disguised.

Baby puppies can be forgiven a slight looseness in front movement and it is possible they will tighten up as they mature. Sensible exercise over a period of time is required, not over-tasking malleable bones with too much exercise too soon, but building up gradually so that by the time they are mature, they have the necessary body fitness and muscle tone to make the most out of what they were born with.

Soundness, while coming from the way the bone structure is in place at birth, also needs to be backed up with exercise so the muscles can support the bone structure and assist the whole body to perform at its maximum efficiency.

Judges can and do place dogs down the line, or out of the cards altogether, which have no muscle tone. A dog required to be "essentially a working terrier" can no more do the job it was bred for if kept too thin and weedy than it can if it is not exercised properly.

It is lovely to go over a dog and feel his muscles hard and firm to the touch. Healthy in mind and healthy in body; a true working breed. You will also reap the rewards of a dog which has had plenty exercise as he will tend to chill out when back at home rather than look for trouble which sometimes stems from boredom. He is happier, you are happier – everyone wins!

The coat on a working dog is one of the most important parts, to withstand a rainy, windy, cold day on the hills around the borders. A dog with thin skin and a single coat would not fare very well or manage for very long out there. The Border should have a double coat, with a waterproof outer coat, being "harsh and dense", lying flat, and a soft, dense undercoat to provide insulation. With the best of coats, they are so tight and the undercoat so close, that when you pull it back you have difficulty seeing the skin. Judges should be checking for this in the show ring.

The Standard advises "skin must be thick". There are not many places where we deviate from "moderate" or "fairly", so we need to pay attention to the word "must" here. Your Border will stay warmer and more able to withstand the rigors of a day in the field and when meeting his adversary underground if he has a thick pliable pelt. Judges who know what to look for, will collect a good handful of pelt and lift it away from the dog to test for this.

Color

There are four colors in the Breed Standard: red, wheaten, grizzle and tan and blue and tan. Red is still seen occasionally, although many more Borders are actually grizzle and tan. Wheaten has not been seen in the breed for over 20 years

All blue and tans are born black, with only a little tan over their eyes, so they look a little like an owl. Grizzle and tan covers a multitude of variations, from very light grizzle to dark red grizzle, but the only official color for all of them is grizzle and tan.

Height and weight

The current Standard asks for dogs of 13 to 15½ lb (6 to 7 kg) and bitches of 11½ to 14 lb (5 to 6.5 kg). There is no height limit to the breed, although

Border Terrier colors:
Blue (left), grizzle
(right).

the old terriermen used a yardstick of an inch to the pound as a rough guide. As time has gone on and standards of care improved, Borders have increased in weight and, in some cases, in height. At the moment, a lot of dogs weigh more than the Standard requires, but if we increased the Standard to match, we might find this resulted in even heavier Borders.

Better to leave the Standard as it is and hope we can get somewhere close to that with the majority of dogs than raise it and find we breed even bigger, heavier dogs.

Faults

The Standard advises: "Any departure from the foregoing points should be considered a fault and the seriousness with which the fault should be regarded should be in exact proportion to its degree, its effect on the terrier's ability to work, and the health and welfare of the dog."

The reference to working ability is one part where the Border Terrier Standard differs from many others, in yet again emphasizing the working traits and attributes of the breed.

Summing up

Although you have probably chosen your Border Terrier as a steadfast friend rather than a show dog, breeders and judges alike should ensure the breed stays true to its roots and without exaggerations.

First and foremost, the Border is a lithe, active, intelligent, healthy dog who should be able to do a day's work if asked. Apart from the otter-like head, this breed is more like a mongrel than many other breeds – and that is no criticism!

What do you want from your Border Terrier?

Some research the breed before they buy, while others only realize it is not the right breed *after* buying – and the poor dog gets all the blame for not fitting in with their exacting requirements. Perhaps dogs should choose the correct owners, as so often humans get it wrong!

Some people expect their dog to just sit there and look the part, and wonder what is wrong if he escapes out of a garden over a 3-foot wall, or becomes deaf to your calls when he picks up an enticing scent when out on a walk. Inevitably, the dog takes the blame for doing what comes naturally, while, in fact, it is the owner that is at fault for not acquiring sufficient knowledge about the breed.

enjoy living in a family with children, or being the devoted companion of owners getting on in years – as long as they remain active.

While he likes a cuddle and will take part in many shared activities,the Border Terrier has a keen intelligence and can have a mind of his own. This is a breed that is quick to learn but can be slow to obey.

Show dog

Do you have ambitions to show your Border Terrier? If this is the case you will need to do a lot of homework, studying the Breed Standard and going to shows so you know what you are looking for.

There is no guarantee that any pup (whatever his qualities at eight weeks or so), will develop into an adult that is good enough to show. A reputable breeder may point out the good and not so good points, but no breeder can guarantee success, even with the puppy they keep themselves. A friend once said he: "put the best to the best and then hoped for the best." You can only make an informed choice then wait to see how your puppy develops as he grows and matures.

What does your Border Terrier want from you?

The Border Terrier is a happy, healthy breed and, in the right hands, his needs are minimal. However, you need to be sure that you can provide the home he needs, otherwise he will be miserable, and may even develop challenging behavioral problems.

No matter the breed, all dogs need a leader they can respect. This is particularly true of intelligent dogs who are quick to follow their own agenda unless directed otherwise. A Border needs to be taught his place in the family pack, and to co-operate with the rules that have been laid down. This does not need to be done by bullying or coercion. A Border responds to positive, reward-based training and, with this, he will fulfil his potential as an outstanding companion.

Exercise

A Border enjoys long walks. An outdoor, rural existence suits him best but, being an adaptable dog, he will also thrive in an urban setting as long as his exercise needs are catered for.

Mental stimulation

A Border Terrier needs more than physical exercise; he also needs mental stimulation. This is an alert, intelligent dog and if he is bored he may find mischief of his own.

Before you get a Border Terrier, you should consider what activities you will enjoy doing together. This could include teaching basic obedience, having a go at agility, or maybe teaching him to be a therapy dog, visiting schools, hospital, or residential homes.

If you do not want to commit to anything too formal, you can invent games to play with your Border, such as playing fetch with a favorite toy, or hide and seek where he searches for a toy hidden in the house.

It is not what you do that matters, it is the principle of spending quality time interacting with your Border Terrier.

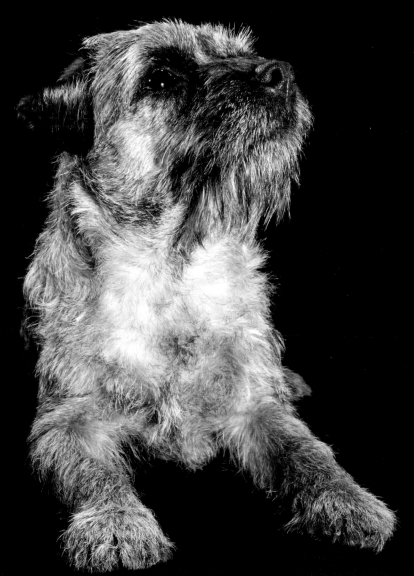

Extra considerations

Now you have decided that the Border Terrier is the breed for you, you need to make some final decisions in order to narrow your search.

Male or female?

Both male and female Borders can be very loving and gentle with their family. But temperament does not come down to gender alone, it is far more dependent on how a puppy has been raised. It is better to find a good breeder who cares for their dogs and brings them up with love and attention than getting hung up about wanting either dog or bitch.

A bitch will come into season twice a year for about three weeks at a time. This should not be a problem so long as properly handled. Carry her to the car, to prevent stray males finding her scent, and then drive to a deserted spot for your walks.

If you do not want to breed from your bitch, you may consider having her spayed. There are health benefits, such as reducing the risk of mammary cancer and womb infections, but it can lead to weight gain and sometimes urinary incontinence. Read as much about the subject as you can and discuss the pros and cons with your vet so you can make an informed decision.

If you choose a male, you may decide to have him castrated. This reduces the risk of testicular cancer, but it should not be seen as a cure-all for behavioral problems such as aggression with other dogs.

If your dog is timid aggressive, reducing his testosterone level may make him more fearful and more aggressive. Again, the best plan is to seek advice from your vet before making a decision.

More than one?

If a breeder is willing to let you have two puppies from the same litter, he is either ignorant or greedy for money! It is never a good idea to buy two pups from the same litter, or even buying two of roughly the same age. If you are thinking they will keep each other company, you should stop and decide if you have enough time for even one puppy. After all, you are supposed to be your puppy's companion!

It is hard enough to train one puppy, but much harder with two, as the pups will pay more attention to each other than to you. If they are opposite sexes, then you will need to keep them apart for three weeks, twice a year. That is problematic to say the least and can result in a male that howls all night!

If they are the same sex, they may reach puberty and decide they want to challenge each other for the top position. You could end up having to keep them apart, defeating the original object of getting two as company. Worse still, you may end up with two dogs or two bitches that are determined to kill each other. Once Borders have fought, you can never trust them alone together.

If you must have two Borders, wait until your first one is about two years old, and choose one of the opposite sex. This

Below: It is better to wait until your first Border is fully established before taking on a second dog.

may mean neutering one, or both, or being prepared to keep them apart for three weeks twice a year, but they are more likely to establish a harmonious relationship.

An older dog

Some people want an older Border because they are getting on in years, or may have a physical disability. Borders continue to be active and love their exercise, generally even into old age.

A dog that is confined in a house can be a problem, so an older Border may not be the right choice for you, unless you can give it plenty of love, care, feeding and exercise for the whole of his life.

Sometimes a breeder will run on a puppy with the hope of showing him, but if he does not quite make the grade, he may be rehomed.

A minor fault, which would be penalized in the show ring, will make absolutely no difference in a pet home, so this is an ideal way of acquiring an older dog. A good breeder will tell you everything about the dog and why it is being re-homed.

Unfortunately, there are a number of Border Terriers who need rehoming through no fault of their own; family break up, moving jobs, or a new baby are all given as reasons when a dog is no longer wanted. You may find a Border Terrier in all-breed rescue centre, but more likely through the rehoming schemes run by breed clubs.

A dog which is looking for a new home as an adult deserves to find a permanent, loving home and not to be passed around, so make sure this is the right dog and right breed for you.

Taking on an older dog can be very rewarding and, the bonus is that, hopefully, the dog will be house trained and beyond the tiresome chewing stage.

However, you need to be patient for the first few weeks as an older dog needs time to get used to a new home. The rescue charity will advise you if you are suitable for the breed and will then try to find a dog which matches your needs.

Sourcing a puppy

Do not be impatient when you start looking for a Border Terrier puppy to buy. Hopefully, your dog will be with you for the next 14 years or more, so it is worth taking your time rather than repenting at leisure.

The best place to start your search is with the Kennel Club website. Both the American Kennel Club (AKC) and the Kennel Club (KC) in the UK have excellent websites with lots of breed specific information. You will be able to find details of breed clubs, and the secretary will let you know of litters in your area. There is also a register of puppies, and if you opt for breeders who have joined the KC scheme (Breeders of Merit in the US; Assured Breeders in the UK), you have the knowledge that they have followed an agreed code of conduct.

Beware of adverts posted on the Internet or in local newspapers. Unless breeders are advertising on their own websites, you cannot find out sufficient information about the dogs that have been produced or how they have been reared. Unfortunately, there are breeders who are only interested in financial gain and care little about the homes their puppies go to.

Questions, questions, questions

When you find a breeder with puppies available, you will have lots of questions to ask. These should include the following:

- Where have the puppies been reared? Hopefully, they will be in a home environment which gives them the best possible start in life.

- How many are in the litter?

- What is the split of males and females?

- How many have already been spoken for?

- Can I see the mother with her puppies?

- What age are the puppies?

- When will they be ready to go to their new homes?

Bear in mind puppies need to be with their mother and siblings until they are eight weeks of age otherwise they miss out on vital learning and

Below: The breeder will want to find out if you can provide a suitable home for a Border Terrier puppy.

communication skills which will have a detrimental effect on them for the rest of their lives.

You should also be prepared to answer a number of searching questions so the breeder can check if you are suitable as a potential owner of one of their precious puppies.

You will be asked some or all of the following questions:

- What is your home set up?
- Is your garden securely fenced?
- Do you have children/grandchildren?
- What are their ages?

- Do you work, and if so how long are you away from home each day?

- What arrangements will be made for your dog when you are at work?

- What is your previous experience with dogs?

- How much exercise will you be able to give your dog?

Judge the breeder by the amount of questions they ask you about your ability to look after their precious puppy. If they are more concerned with telling you how much the puppy costs before asking you any questions about your lifestyle or household, then walk away!

Health issues

The Border Terrier suffers from few hereditary problems and there are no health tests required for breeding stock at the moment. However, you would be advised to talk to the breeder about the health status of their dogs and find out if there are any issues of concern.

Facing page: You will need to check out the family's history, particularly in relation to health issues.

Puppy
watching

Puppies are irresistible – and Border Terrier puppies perhaps more so any other breed. They have so much character, and they are so full of fun, you will probably want to take the whole litter home with you.

However, try not to let your heart rule your head; listen to the breeder who will have picked out all the individual personalities in the litter.

The essentials

Before you decide to buy a puppy, make sure you are happy with the way the litter has been reared, and the general health of the litter. Look out for the following:

- A clean, hygienic environment.

- Puppies who are out-going and friendly, and eager to meet you. Even if some are a little quieter than others, they may well blossom in their new home.

- A sweet-natured mother who is ready to show off her pups.

- Puppies that are well covered, but not pot-bellied, which could be an indication of worms

- Bright eyes, with no sign of soreness or discharge

- Clean ears that smell fresh

- No discharge from the nose

- Clean rear ends – matting could indicate upset tummies

- Lively pups that are keen to play.

Pet home

Make sure the breeder knows all about your family/ home set up so there is the best chance of making a good match. If you have children, it is a good idea to being them along so you can see how the puppies interact with them.

Bear in mind that temperament and health are your top priorities. A puppy may have a minor fault, such as ears that are too big, which means he is not suitable for the show ring. However, this is of absolutely no importance in a pet home as long as the puppy is sound in mind and body and has a temperament that is likely to suit your lifestyle.

Show puppy

It takes an expert to look at a puppy of eight weeks, or so, and work out if it has show potential. If you are looking for a show puppy, make sure the breeder knows that this is what you want. It is in their interests to make sure that only the best of the dogs they produce are exhibited in the ring. It is also advisable to enlist the help of someone who is experienced in the breed who will be able to give an objective opinion.

A good otter-like head is important as is decent, but not too much, bone, straight front and good movement. Look for a strong neck flowing into good narrow ribs with level topline and a well-set tail, thick at the base and tapering.

Look for a good scissor bite, even in puppy teeth. This can later become undershot when teeth change, but an undershot mouth at eight weeks is likely to remain undershot when adult teeth come through, so best to start out with it right!

Similarly, a pup with a snipey muzzle is not going to suddenly have a good head when an adult, although a promising head can develop into a bad head when the pup matures. So do the best you can to buy from the best you can.

A Border Terrier friendly home

You need to plan ahead before you collect your pup, so you have all the equipment, food and toys ready for your new arrival. You will also need to make sure your home and garden are safe and secure. These preparations apply to a new puppy but, in reality, they are the means of creating an environment that is safe and secure for your Border Terrier throughout his life.

Safety in the home

It is essential that you make your house and garden safe and remove any potential hazards. A pup unsupervised for even a moment can pull or knock

things off low tables, get into cupboards or out through doors.

Fit secure catches on cupboards to keep cleaning fluids and other toxic substances out of reach, and use baby-gates on external doors and on the stairs to give an extra safety net.

Make sure that all electric wires are secured out of reach, as these are potentially lethal. Bitter Apple spray can be applied to woodwork and other chair legs which will help prevent chewing. If you have anything that you value, that is easily breakable, move it well out of the way or move it into a puppy free zone.

Check the fencing in the garden, and make sure there are no small gaps in the hedge or fence or behind the garden shed that could provide an escape route.

Dogs grow rapidly and you will need to update your proofing as your pup matures.

Buying equipment

Before your pup arrives, you will need to decide what equipment to buy:

Indoor crate

A crate acts as a cosy den; it makes a puppy feel safe and secure, and it encourages bladder control since dogs do not like to urinate in their sleeping quarters. You can use bedding in the back half of the crate and place newspaper in the front half as, initially, a puppy will not be able to go throughout the night without spending. The crate has added benefits of being a safe place for a pup to rest. It will give him a break from children in the house, and when you leave him, you will not return to a house that the dog has destroyed through anxiety.

Make sure you buy a crate that is big enough for your Border Terrier when he is fully grown – ideally 3 ft long x 2 ft high x 2 ft wide (900 cm x 600 cm x 600 cm) – as this will

probably remain his preferred sleeping quarters.

Many owners use a crate for traveling in the car. If you decide to do this, use one of a slightly smaller size.

Bedding

You can use synthetic fleece bedding inside the crate or in the house, but not bean bags or wicker beds, as they can easily be chewed, posing a potential hazard to your puppy if swallowed. The advantage of synthetic fleece is that is easy to wash and quick to dry. You will need at least three pieces so you can rotate them when they need washing.

Toys

Border Terriers love playing with toys, but they can be quite destructive so you will need to choose with care. Avoid soft toys, or those made of soft plastic which can be easily chewed. Instead, go for hard toys or kongs, which can be stuffed with food.

Tug of war games can damage teeth or make the dog think he is in charge if he wins the tug. Never allow small children to play such games with your dog unattended; if the dog tries to grab the tug, he may bite the child by mistake and he should not pay the ultimate price for your poor choice of toys and lack of supervision.

Small puppies will enjoy ripping apart cardboard boxes or playing with an old sock, or plastic bottle. All fine, but never leave them unattended with any of those things, as they could result in blocked intestines or choking, both of which can be fatal.

A dog is not capable of distinguishing between an old sock and a new one, or an old slipper and your best pair of expensive leather boots! Keep anything you don't want chewed out of his way, with doors closed. Blame yourself if he finds something to chew as it's your fault!

Bowls

Use non-spill water bowls in the house, changing the water many times each day. We use circular feeding bowls. Stainless steel bowls are best, as anything else can be chewed (plastic) or broken (ceramic).

Food

The breeder should provide you with a diet sheet and hopefully a small supply of food. Ask in advance what type of food is being used; do not change the diet just for the sake of it, or your puppy may develop diarrhoea. If you must change, wait a few weeks then make the change gradually over a period of a week.

Collar and lead

Use a puppy collar and lead for the first few weeks, but never leave the collar on your puppy if he is unsupervised, as it could get snagged on something.

Make sure you have the right size collar on your Border, checking it is sufficiently tight so you can only get one or two fingers between the collar and the neck.

We mostly use leather collars and leads for our adult dogs, but providing the lead is the right length and safe, any of the softer ones will do the job.

Grooming gear

How much grooming equipment you need to get will depend on whether you intend to hand strip your Border Terrier, or whether you plan to use the services of a grooming parlour.

However, at the very least you should buy a stiff bristle brush and a comb so your puppy can get used to being groomed. These will also help to remove dirt and debris from the adult coat.

Tiny pups can be kept fresh with unscented baby wipes, while adult Borders who like to roll can be cleaned with water, baby wipes, or tea tree oil wipes sold in pet stores.

ID

We now have all pups micro-chipped before they leave for their new homes and all our adults are micro-chipped. If your breeder has not had your puppy chipped, please consider having your own vet do it as soon as possible. If your Border should escape from your garden, or be stolen, the microchip may enable his safe return home. It is a legal requirement for your dog to have an identity disc with your contact details, which can be attached to the collar.

Finding a vet

Before you pick up your pup, you need to find a vet.
Look in your local directory or online, talk to friends
who are dog owners and take advice from your
puppy's breeder. If you make an appointment with
the vet at this point, you can arrange for your
pup to have a complete check up within
three days of purchase.

Settling in

Arriving in a new home is a daunting prospect, no matter how confident your puppy appears to be. Be patient with him and work at establishing a routine which will help to ease the transition.

Arrange to collect your puppy in the morning so he has the rest of the day to get used to his new home. First of all, take him to the garden, staying with him while he explores. He will probably relieve himself, so be on hand to give him lots of praise.

Next take him into the house and show him his indoor crate. You can encourage him to go in and investigate by throwing a couple of treats in there for him. At mealtimes, feed your puppy in his crate and this will help to build up a good association.

Meeting the family

If there are children at home, they are bound to be excited but try to keep things as calm as possible. Do not let them pick the puppy up; instead, ask them to sit on the floor and let him come to them. If there

is more than one child, make sure they do not fight over who holds him next!

All small puppies have needle-sharp teeth, and they will have used them playing with their littermates. However, this is not acceptable behavior when a pup is interacting with his human family and must be discouraged from day one. If the puppy nips, the best plan is to distract him with a toy – something he is allowed to play with. He will grow out of it, usually by about four to five months, if you adopt this procedure right from the start

When your puppy is tired, make sure he goes into his crate and is allowed to rest. Puppies need a lot of sleep, and if they are deprived of this they will become fractious.

The animal family

If you have a resident dog, you will need to supervise interactions until they establish their own relationship. Allow them to meet in garden and don't worry if the adult puts the puppy in his place as that is the natural order of things. It is very rare that an adult dog will seriously harm a small puppy, but you need to be on hand to encourage and reassure the older dog.

If the adult pins the puppy down, the pup should submit. This is normal adult dominance, so let it happen and try not to interfere, unless the adult is actually harming the puppy. Do not drag the older dog away, telling him off, as you are messing with the natural order. The adult dog should be the boss, although of course, you are the boss of both!

Feed them apart at first, and do not let them share sleeping quarters until you trust them totally together. If they are crated at night, each dog should always have his own crate.

If you have a cat, your Border can learn to live with it, if introduced at an early age under supervision. Make sure the cat can escape out of the way of a pesky puppy if it wishes, otherwise the cat might resort to physical retaliation – and cat's claws and puppy eyes do not mix.

The first night

Do not leave your puppy in a large room on his own for the first time in his life. That can be quite frightening for a small puppy and may be the reason he cries pitifully all night. It is much kinder to confine him to a small space in a room, ideally in a crate, rather than allowing him to wander.

If he falls asleep during the day, put him in his crate and let him sleep alone. He will be much more likely

to settle at night if he knows the scenery, the bed smells familiar, and knows you come back when he wakes.

It is inevitable that he will cry to begin with as he will miss the company of his littermates. However, it is best to harden your heart so he gets used to the routine and does not think that every time he protests, you come running. If he is warm and cosy, and feels safe and secure, he will learn to settle.

House rules

If a puppy is to behave in the way you want, he needs to learn what is 'acceptable' behavior. He does not arrive knowing instinctively what is right or wrong – you have to teach him, rewarding the behavior you want so he is more likely to repeat it.

Before your puppy arrives, you and your family should decide on what the puppy is – and is not – allowed to do, then you must all stick to the rules. For example, if you decide, he is not to go on the furniture, this means he never goes on the furniture – not even when he is curled up on a cushion and looks irresistibly sweet! However, if you are happy to let your Border sleep on the sofa or your bed, he will not object!

House training

Your puppy will usually get the idea of what is required within the first few days.

The best plan is to allocate a toileting area in your garden and take your puppy to this spot every time he needs to relieve himself. He will quickly build up an association and will know why you have brought him out to the garden.

Establish a routine and make sure you take your puppy out at the following times:

- First thing in the morning

- After mealtimes

- On waking from a sleep

- Following a play session

- Last thing at night.

A puppy should be taken out to relieve himself every two hours as an absolute minimum. An hourly trip out to the garden is even better.

The more often your puppy gets it 'right', the quicker he will be clean in the house. It helps if you use a verbal cue, such as "Busy", when your pup is performing. In time, this will trigger the desired response.

Do not be tempted to put your puppy out on the doorstep on his own in the hope that he will toilet. Most pups simply sit there, waiting to get back inside the house! No matter how bad the weather is, accompany your puppy and give him lots of praise when he performs correctly.

Do not rush back inside as soon as he has finished. Your puppy might start to delay in the hope of prolonging his time outside with you. Praise him, have a quick game – and then you can both return indoors.

When accidents happen

No matter how vigilant you are, there are bound to be accidents. If you witness the accident, never scold him. Just take your puppy outside immediately, and give him lots of praise if he finishes his business out there.

If you are not there when he has an accident, do not scold him when you finally do see what has happened. He will not remember what he has done and will not understand why his owner is so cross.

Use a deodorizer when you clean up, so your pup is not tempted to use the same spot again. Remember, vigilance is the key to effective house training, and the fewer mistakes your puppy makes, the quicker he will learn to be clean in the house.

Choosing a diet

"We are what we eat" applies to dogs as much as to people. Feeding can have a big impact, not only on size, shape, stomach, bowels and skin condition, but also on his mental wellbeing.

There are many ways to feed a dog, be it raw, processed, tinned or dried food, or your own preparations; not all dogs will thrive on the same diet. Find one that suits your dog and stick to it, until either his age or a medical condition make change necessary.

Natural diets

Some people feed a raw food diet to their dogs to mimic the diet of wolves or wild dog packs, giving raw meat and bones in a certain percentage of each over a couple of weeks. There are pros and cons with this diet, so consult your vet or use the Internet to research it thoroughly before going ahead.

Canned food

This type of 'wet' food is available in cans, trays or pouches, and can be fed on its own or with biscuit. Most dogs find it very appetizing, and it can be useful if you are tempting a dog to eat after an illness.

However, if you are feeding it on a permanent basis, you need to make sure it is at least 60 per cent meat, has no additives or artificial preservatives and no grains, such as wheat or barley, which can cause irritation to skin and/or bowels.

Complete

Complete diets, which come in the form of dry kibble, are the most popular, and most convenient method of feeding. Most brands are tailored to life stage feeding – puppy, adult maintenance and senior – and there are also special diets for breeding bitches, as well as prescription diets for dogs with specific health problems.

We tend to think a complete diet looks boring, and so we are tempted to add extras to it. However, this type of diet is specially manufactured to cater for all nutritional needs and the balance can be upset if it is supplemented.

As with all diets, fresh drinking water should be freely available.

Feeding regime

A puppy should be on four meals a day at eight weeks of age. At around five months of age, we change to three meals a day and then cut down to two meals a day by about seven months.

We find that Borders are generally ready to change from puppy to adult food by five to six months of age. From then onwards we stick to a regime of feeding twice daily, varying mealtimes slightly so the dogs do not get too set in a routine.

Ideal weight

The Breed Standard sets weights for the ideal Border Terrier, but you should not try to achieve those weights without due regard to your own dog. Some dogs are taller and rangier than others and to try to get a dog like that down to the weight in the Standard would require half-starving him.

You should be able to feel the ribs slightly but should never be able to feel them protruding or see the backbone sticking up.

A puppy should have sufficient bodyweight so that if he falls ill, he has something to fall back on. I hate to see a six-month-old puppy with his ribs sticking out. Make sure he is well covered – not roly-poly fat, but his ribs should not be visible.

Sometimes people see a fat distended belly and think a puppy is well fed, when he actually has worms.

Make sure when you purchase your puppy that he has been wormed at least three times before you take him (usually every two weeks from two to three weeks old), then continue to worm him on your vet's advice.

At the other end of the scale you need to be aware of the dangers of obesity which can lead to major health problems.

Do not get hung up about the amount of food recommended by the manufacturer, but feed the appropriate amount for your dog, depending on his stage of life and his activity level.

Below: You can cut down to three meals a day when your Border is around five months of age.

Beware when your Border is in full coat. Underneath that hairy, heavy-looking dog may be a starving Border. Don't wait until he has been hand-stripped to realize it; check him weekly. Too fat? Reduce food gradually. Too thin? Increase food gradually. Getting older? Might need a different type of food.

Watch the number of additions to his diet, such as treats he is given each day. If you are using treats for training, you will need to take this on board and reduce the amount you give your Border at mealtimes.

Bones and chews

Never give weight-bearing bones such as knuckle bones; they can fracture your dog's teeth. Raw ribs of beef or lamb and raw chicken wings, given under supervision, are the best. Never give cooked bones as these can splinter in the gut or intestines causing fatal damage.

We never give chew sticks made of hide; Borders are so greedy, they can try to swallow them whole, or chew off large, indigestible pieces, which can cause blockages.

Caring for your Border Terrier

Your Border looks to you for his health and happiness and will reward you ten-fold for the love and attention you give him.

Grooming

A Border's daily grooming needs are a quick brush and comb and he is good to go. However, his coat will need to be stripped twice a year. Some pet owners opt for the services of a professional groomer, but you will need to decide if you want the coat hand-stripped or clipped.

Hand-stripping does take time, but the advantage is that the topcoat will retain its harsh texture when it grows back in and help to keep the undercoat clean and dry, so enabling the undercoat to do its job of keeping the dog warm. This is essential whether your Border is a pet, a show dog or a working dog.

When a Border Terrier's coat is ready to strip, you should be able to extract the hairs from the top of his back, just in front of the tail end, by pulling them in the direction they grow. If his hair comes out easily on the back of his neck, but not so easily from his haunches, he is not ready to be stripped yet.

Some experienced show exhibitors 'roll' the coat, taking about one-seventh of the coat out every two weeks. This ensures that the correct amount is removed, and the Border retains his typical rugged appearance, but with a smooth outline that will enhance his appearance.

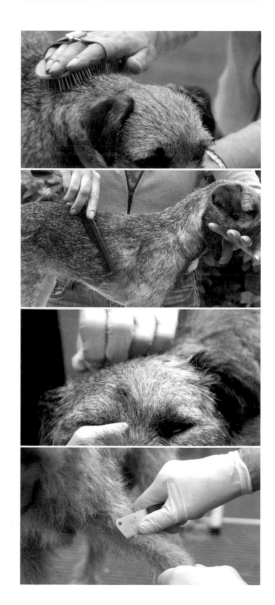

Start by brushing the coat.

Next, go through the coat with a comb.

The coat is stripped by plucking out the hair using finger and thumb.

A stripping knife will aid the process.

Bathing

Borders like to roll in foul-smelling droppings and they also like racing around in a field of wet mud. In most cases, the mud will drop off when the dog is dry, but odors are not so easy to remove.

Do not bath your Border more than strictly necessary, as it softens the texture of his coat. However, it is a good idea to accustom him to the procedure from an early age so he does not kick up a fuss.

Regular checks

Weekly checks will keep your Border in tip-top condition, and if something is wrong you will spot it at an early stage so you can seek help, or sort it out, before it becomes too much of a problem.

Teeth

Examine your Border's teeth and, if there is tartar build-up, clean using a soft toothbrush or finger-stall and dog toothpaste. Never use human toothpaste.

When your puppy is teething, at four to five months, check his mouth regularly to make sure his adult canines come through in the right place. Sometimes milk teeth do not come out when they should. The adult canines can grow on the inside of these, into the roof of his mouth. If in doubt, consult your vet.

Teeth cleaning will prevent the build up of tartar.

Ears should be clean and smell fresh.

Debris from the eyes can be wiped away.

Nails will need to be trimmed on a routine basis.

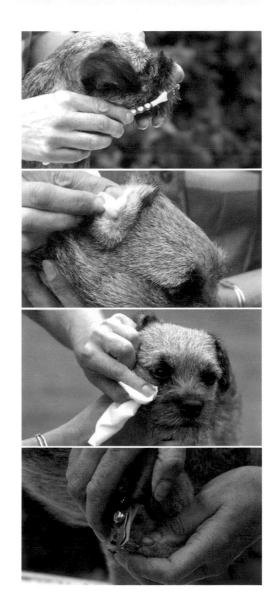

Ears

Check your Border's ears weekly and if they are dirty or smelly, you can clean the outside of the ear with a liquid cleaner which you can get from your vet. As your dog can suffer from canker or ear mites, it is best to let the vet have a look if your dog's ears continue to be dirty or foul smelling.

Ticks will sometimes attach themselves to warm places on the dog, the inside of the ear being a good hiding place. So, if you walk in a tick-infested area, check your dog's ears after each walk.

Nails

Nails should be clipped regularly from puppyhood so your Border gets used to the procedure. Make sure you do not cut the quick (the blood vessel in the nail, which does not extend right to the tip). If you can clip a little off the end of the nail each week, you will help to keep the quick away from the end of the nail, thereby reducing the risk of cutting into it.

Exercise regimes

As already noted, the Border Terrier is a dog that needs plenty of varied exercise to keep him fit and well. However, do not get carried away and take a puppy on lengthy walks. While he is growing, exercise should be given in moderation. Initially, a

puppy will get as much exercise as he needs playing in the garden. When you start lead training, you can give him short outings which will form part of his socialization program. Free running should be allowed in short bursts only – assuming you have taught your Border a reliable recall – and then stepped up as he becomes fully mature.

The older Border

There are so many books about how to raise and train a puppy and few about caring for the older dog. With age can come arthritis, confusion, and problems with sight, hearing, continence and mobility. It behoves us to look out for the signs and ask the vet for advice if we think there is something wrong.

Make sure your older Border does not become obese, but also that any weight gain or loss, and changes in bodily functions are brought to the vet's attention. There are many things we can do to make an older dog's life more pleasant and we owe it to him to do our best. Your Border should be able to enjoy daily walks with you as he gets older, but you may have to shorten the walk a little or consider putting him on a flexi lead in the field or park, if his sight and/or hearing have deteriorated.

Be aware of the changing needs of your Border Terrier as he grows older.

If your Border starts to have problems with his digestion, you may need to tweak his diet a little. There are commercial diets for older dogs on the market, which are easier to digest, or you could cook chicken or fish (with rice) for him. If he has arthritis, you may need tablets or some form of additive to help his joints, but always under the help and guidance of your vet.

A young Border may give an older one a new lease of life, but don't let the youngster push him about. Don't forget to interact with your old dog yourself. If you play with him a little, in a gentle way, you may find he makes more contact with you and seeks you out more, rather than just sleeping in his basket. Although he may sleep more than a young mature dog, he still needs to be a much-loved member of your family.

Letting go

There is much that modern veterinary medicine can do to prolong life and make our dogs' old age easier and, of course, we must give them their chance and heal them if it can be done. But it is wrong to keep old dogs going when clearly they are suffering. The last act of kindness is to let him go with dignity. Anne Roslin-Williams of the Mansergh Border Terriers once wrote something along the lines of:

"Rather a day too soon than a day too late", and that has stuck in my mind ever since.

When you feel the time has come, discuss it with your vet, who may be able to help you come to a decision by telling you what he can and cannot do. But it is always going to be your decision. You must not be selfish, wanting him to stay because you don't want to lose him. He gave you love, comfort and loyalty all the time you had him. Now repay him and take away his pain.

Parting is always heartbreaking but, in time, you will be able to look back on all the happy times you spent with your beloved Border.

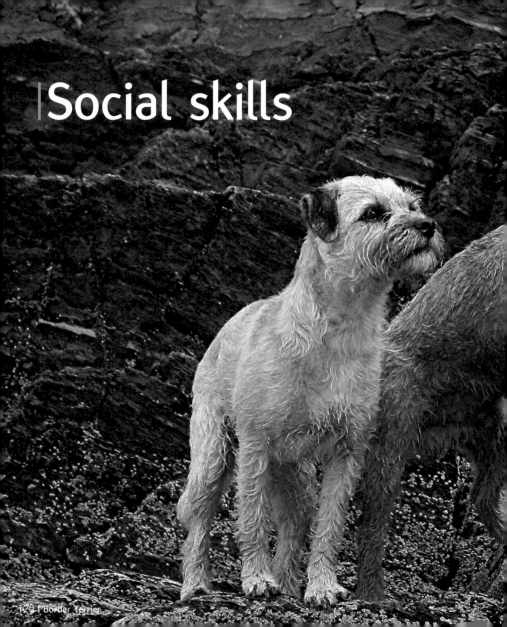

Social skills

Your puppy's breeder should have started the process of socialization, equipping him to deal with new situations with calmness and confidence. This will be the foundation of how he views the word, and it is your job to continue the work so that he matures into a happy, adaptable adult.

Early weeks

In the first few weeks, a bitch should have time to bond with her puppies quietly. Changing bedding frequently and weighing them every other day is sufficient interference at this time. In this way, she may suckle her puppies more frequently than one kept in a busy, noisy room.

When the pups are about three weeks old, breeders move the puppy pen into the family room, gradually introducing other dogs, with everything done to make the bitch happy and relaxed. If a bitch is tense, the pups become tense themselves, which is why you should always breed from a bitch with a sound temperament.

Hearing normal household activity at this stage helps the puppies when they move to a new home environment.

Making progress

From about four weeks, breeders may welcome visitors, but supervise all interaction, making sure the puppies are not harmed or worried and that everyone stays calm around them.

Taking over

At eight to twelve weeks of age, the puppies are probably going to their new homes. Although your pup cannot go out until he has had all his vaccinations, it is important that his socialization is continued, but at a slow pace so he does not become overwhelmed.

You can accustom your puppy to traveling in the car, and taking him out and about, even though you will have to carry him. Remember, an unvaccinated puppy is very vulnerable so avoid making contact with people, or putting him on the ground.

Once your puppy has completed his vaccinations, you can venture further afield. Start off in quiet places, and build up to busier places, with heavier traffic, as your puppy's confidence increases. Never drag your puppy along on the end of the lead; you can use a treat to encourage him, and make sure you remain calm and confident so that he knows there is nothing to worry about.

Socializing Borders with other dogs

It is important that your puppy has good experiences with dogs of sound temperament in his early days. One bad experience in the park can affect your Border for the rest of his life. Try to meet up with a friend who has a calm dog, making the first few walks a pleasant experience.

Puppy parties, where lots of breeds of different sizes and temperaments are allowed off-lead, is not recommended for the Border Terrier; if he has a nasty experience with a breed he may end up disliking all dogs of that breed in the future.

If you go to a training class, first go without your dog, see how the trainers interact with the dogs, check if they have any experience with terriers and, if you don't like what you see, find another class. Some trainers are more used to training large guarding breeds and the methods used to train them may not always suit Border Terriers.

Do:

- Let your puppy socialize with other vaccinated dogs of different ages, sizes and breeds, but ensure all are on leads and supervised.

- Keep your dog's lead relaxed around other dogs. Talk softly to him and watch carefully the body language of all the dogs. If you feel another dog is becoming aggressive with yours, distract your puppy with a treat or a toy and move quietly away from the other one (not pulling him away or tightening the lead).

- Praise all positive interaction with other dogs and continue the socialization on a regular basis.

Don't:

- Pick your dog up when another dog comes over; he may become fearful and aggressive. The other dog may also start to jump up at you and you could be bitten.

- Let other dogs harass or intimidate your dog. Borders do not like to have large dogs looming over them.

- Let your puppy off the lead with dogs you are unsure of. You will have no control if something goes wrong.

- Introduce your pup to other dogs in their territory. Always choose somewhere away from food, beds or toys and on neutral territory.

- Take your Border to puppy parties, where dogs of all ages are allowed to interact off the lead.

On-going socialization

Training and socialization are the building blocks for a steady and calm dog. Not all training methods work with all dogs, so find what works for your dog and if at first you don't succeed, work on finding a different method.

Training guidelines

Border Terriers are loving dogs in the right hands, but can be easily upset and never need harsh correction. By using a reward-based method of training, you can channel your Border's energies into positive actions and away from any destructive or unwanted behavior.

Training has the benefits of:

• Forming a strong bond between you and your dog.

• Emphasizing your role as the pack leader.

• Stimulating the mind. Your dog will love to learn new things as well as just being with you, interacting with you, and being rewarded with affection and/or food.

When you start training, follow the guidelines below which will give you the best chance of success:

- Find a reward your Border Terrier really wants. This could be a toy or food, depending on the individual.

- If you are using food, you can vary the reward so you have high value treats (cheese or sausage) for teaching new exercises and recalls away from home, and low value treats (dry kibble) for routine training.

- If you are using a toy as a reward, make sure you only bring it out for training sessions so it has added value.

- Work on your tone of voice. This will be far more meaningful to your Border than the words you are saying. Use a bright, happy, upbeat tone when you are training, and a deep, firm voice when you catch him red handed – raiding the bin, for example. Go over the top when you praising your Border so that he understands how pleased you are with him.

- Train in short sessions. This applies particularly to puppies, which have a very short attention span. Adults will also switch off if sessions are too long.

- Never train if you are preoccupied or if you are in a bad mood. Your Border will pick up your negative vibes, and the session is doomed to failure.

- Teach one lesson at a time and only proceed to the next lesson when the first has been mastered.

- Praise success lavishly and ignore failure. You do not have to tell your dog off if he gets it wrong. Simply ignore what he has done, and use a bright, positive tone of voice and tell him to "Try again".

- If your Border is struggling with an exercise, break it down into stages so you can reward him at every step, and he has a clearer understanding of what is required.

- Make sure training sessions always end on a positive note – even if this means abandoning an exercise for the time being and finishing with something you know your Border can do.

- Above all, make sure your training sessions are fun, with lots of play and plenty of opportunities to reward you dog, so that you both enjoy spending time together.

First lessons

A puppy has so much to learn, and it is much better that he learns good manners rather than trying to break bad habits at a later stage. The golden rule is to be consistent so your puppy understands what is expected of him.

Wearing a collar

When you first bring your puppy home and have got to know each other, accustom him to wearing a soft puppy collar for a few minutes.

Fit the collar so that you can get at least two fingers between the collar and his neck. Then have a game to distract his attention.

This will work for a few moments; then he will stop, put his back leg up behind his neck and scratch away at the peculiar, itchy thing round his neck, which feels so odd.

Bend down, rotate the collar, pat him on the head and distract him by gently throwing a toy for him

to retrieve. Once he has worn the collar for a few minutes each day, he will soon ignore it and become used to it.

Remember, never leave the collar on the puppy unsupervised, especially when he is outside in the garden.

Walking on the lead

Once your puppy is used to the collar, take him outside into your secure garden where there are no distractions.

Attach the lead and, to begin with, allow him to wander with the lead trailing, making sure it does not become snarled up. Then pick up the lead and follow the pup where he wants to go; he needs to get used to the sensation of being attached to you.

The next stage is to get your Border to follow you, and for this you will need some tasty treats. You can show him a treat in your hand, and then encourage him to follow you. Walk a few paces, and if he is wco-operating, stop and reward him.

If he puts on the brakes, simply change direction and lure him with the treat – it does not take a Border long to realize that if he co-operates, a treat will follow.

Next, introduce some changes of direction so your puppy is walking confidently alongside you. At this stage, introduce a verbal cue "Heel" when your puppy is in the correct position.

Do not work at this exercise for too long; your puppy will find it hard to concentrate. The best plan is to accomplish a short distance of good lead walking and then reward him with a treat, and maybe a game with his favorite toy.

You can then graduate to walking your puppy away from your home – as long as he has completed his vaccination program – starting in quiet areas and building up to busier environments.

If your puppy tries to pull on the lead, do not try to pull him back into position – he will think this is all part of a game. Simply come to a halt, ask your puppy to "Heel" and then move forward again, rewarding him when he is in the correct position.

If he persists in pulling, stop and walk in the opposite direction. Your Border needs to learn pulling gets him nowhere – he only makes progress when he is walking on a loose lead.

Come when called

Teaching a reliable recall is invaluable for both you and your Border Terrier. This is a terrier with an acute sense of smell and a strong prey drive, so every walk is full of exciting opportunities. You need to work on your recall so you are secure in the knowledge that he will come back when he is called – even though he may take longer than you wish...

Getting started

The breeder will have started recall training simply by calling the puppies at mealtimes and this is an excellent start as they will have built up a positive response to being called.

When your puppy arrives in his new home, he will feel a little lost and lonely, and he will follow you everywhere. Capitalise on this by stopping every so often, and calling your pup, using his name.

Make sure you have a treat so you can reward him when he comes to you. You can also do this at mealtimes, asking your pup to "Come" when his dinner is ready.

The next stage is to transfer the lesson to the garden. Arm yourself with some treats, and wait until your puppy is distracted. Then call him, using a higher-pitched, excited tone of voice. If your puppy responds, immediately reward him with a treat.

If he is slow to come, run away a few steps and then call again, making yourself sound really exciting. Jump up and down, open your arms wide to welcome him; it doesn't matter how silly you look, he needs to see you as the most fun person in the world.

Now you are ready to introduce some distractions. Try calling him when someone else is in the garden, or wait a few minutes until he is investigating a really interesting scent.

When he responds, make a really big fuss of him and give him some extra treats so he knows it is worth his while to come to you.

Venturing further afield

When you have a reliable recall in the garden, you can venture into the outside world. Do not be too ambitious to begin with; try a recall on a quiet place with the minimum of distractions and only progress to more challenging environments if your Border is responding well.

If you are not secure in his recall, use a long training lead or an extending flexi-lead. A lot of well-trained Borders can become deaf when their noses are filled with the scent of prey, so it is always better to be safe than sorry.

Stationary exercises

The Sit and Down are easy to teach, and will give you a basic level of control. You can then progress to the Stay exercise.

Sit

The best method is to lure your Border into position, and for this you can use a treat, a toy, or his food bowl. Simply hold the reward above his head. As he looks up, he will lower his hindquarters and go into a sit.

Practice this a few times and when your puppy understands what you are asking, introduce the verbal cue "Sit".

Down

This is an important lesson, and can be a lifesaver if an emergency arises and you need to bring your Border to an instant halt.

You can start with your dog in a Sit or a Stand for this exercise. Stand or kneel in front of him and show him you have a treat in your hand.

Hold the treat just in front of his nose and slowly lower it towards the ground, between his front legs. As he follows the treat he will go down on his front legs and, in a few moments, his hindquarters will follow.

Close your hand over the treat so your Border doesn't cheat and get the treat before he is in the correct position. As soon as he is in the Down, give him the treat and lots of praise.

Keep practising, and when your Border understands what you want, introduce the verbal cue "Down".

If your Border is a little reluctant to go into position, you can apply gentle pressure on his shoulders to encourage him.

With both these exercises, you are effectively luring your dog into the correct position. When he understands the exercise, you can drop the lure, and use the verbal cue on its own. It is a good idea to reward him every now and again, just to keep him guessing.

Control exercises

There are times when you need to stop your puppy in his tracks – this may be because he is misbehaving in some way, or it may be because he is doing something that is potentially dangerous. Whatever the reason, you want to teach your Border an instant response.

Teaching "No" and "Leave"

If the puppy is doing something bad and you want it to stop, use "No", in a deep, authoritative tone, not a high-pitched, soft voice. Combine that with your own body language, shoulders squared so you feel in command. Take a step towards the puppy, watching carefully for his reaction as some are more easily frightened than others and a brief "No" might be all that is required.

No" means stop that now, but if you merely wish your puppy to leave something alone, teach the command "Leave" or "Give", by offering praise or a treat for what has been relinquished. This works when throwing a ball for the puppy. "Give" is followed by throwing the ball – result for both human and puppy!

"Wait"

You can teach "Wait" when puppy brings a ball back to you. Say "Wait", putting the ball in one hand and holding the other hand up, arm outstretched and palm facing him. At this point, your pup may freeze, waiting for you to throw the ball. When he is waiting quietly, throw the ball – and your pup receives the reward for waiting, learning through play.

Similarly, when you are feeding them, hold the food bowl in one hand, other arm outstretched as described above, saying "Wait". Combining the Sit command, and add "Wait" just before you put the bowl on the ground.

You can also teach a release command, so your Border knows he is free to eat his food. I use the word "OK", but anything consistent will do, so long as your Border knows you are in control – then leave him in peace to feed.

Once he has learned to "Wait" at play and at mealtimes, you can teach him that "Wait" also applies to other situations, such as before the door is open to go for a walk, or before crossing a road, or before you clip on his lead when he gets out of the car. But do not risk injury or death by allowing your Border out of the house or car before clipping on his lead.

"Stay"

You need to differentiate this exercise from the "Wait" by using a different hand signal and a different verbal cue. While " Wait" means stay still until the next command is given, "Stay" means stay in position for a period of some duration, until the release command is given.

Start with your Border in the Down as he most likely to be secure in this position. Stand by his side and then step forwards, with your hand held back, palm facing the dog.

Step back, release him, and then reward him. Practice until your Border understands the exercise and then introduce the verbal cue "Stay".

Gradually increase the distance you can leave your puppy, and increase the challenge by walking around him – and even stepping over him – so that he learns he must "Stay" until you release him.

It is easier to teach your Border to "Stay" when he is in the Down position.

The ideal owner

A dog deserves to have an owner who understands how the canine mind works and tries to use the most natural training techniques, which are easy to understand. A Border also deserves to have an owner who understands a working terrier...

A Border Terrier might wish his owner would be one who will:

- Not mind if he rolls in or eats fox dirt – or anything else he finds attractive

- Nor if he rips the fence out to get to the rodent on the other side, but who will make the fence escape proof before he gets out.

- Understand when he chases a rabbit.

- Love his cute little otter-like face and enjoy cuddles on the settee, but make sure he has enough exercise for mind and body.

- Not try to make him fit exactly the weight stated in the Breed Standard, but feeds him sufficient food for his size, making sure he is well covered but not fat.

- Take him to the vet when he is ill or injured.

- Teach him commands but understand he can be easily upset by a harsh word and never uses physical punishment, or loses his temper.

- Be forgiving if things are chewed which owners should have put away.

- Think again about buying a Border if he does not have the time or energy to look after one properly.

- Understand that he is "essentially a working terrier"!

Opportunities for Border Terriers

If you are enjoying training your Border Terrier you may want to get involved in more advanced training, or take part in one of the many canine sports on offer.

Good citizen scheme

The Good Citizen Scheme is run by the national Kennel Clubs in both the USA and the UK, and is designed to promote responsible ownership and to teach basic obedience and good manners so your dog is a model citizen in the community. In the US there is one test; in the UK there are four award levels: Puppy Foundation, Bronze, Silver and Gold.

Agility

This is great fun to watch and join in. Against the clock, at the fastest speed they can muster, dogs jump over obstacles, through tires and tunnels, and negotiate the contact equipment, which includes an A frame, a dog walk and a seesaw.

The Border Terrier is quick-witted and can move at speed, so most do very well in this sport. The key is to find a focus, such as a favorite toy – preferably one he can 'kill' – so he is motivated to work for you.

Obedience

If your Border Terrier has mastered basic obedience, you may want to get involved in competitive obedience. The exercises include: heelwork at varying paces with dog and handler following a pattern decided by the judge, stays, recalls, retrieves, sendaways, scent discrimination and distance control. The exercises get progressively harder as you progress up the classes.

A Border will readily learn the exercises that are used in obedience competitions, but, at the top level, a very high degree of precision and accuracy is called for.

Earthdog trials

The American Kennel Club run earthdog trials which are specifically designed to test the working ability

of various breeds of dog, including the small-legged terriers that were bred to "go to ground" in search of quarry. Man-made tunnels are created, and the dog must work the tunnels in order to find the quarry, which he will indicate by barking, whining, scratching, or digging. The quarry (usually two rats) are protected by wooden bars across the end of the tunnel so they are not endangered. The Border Terrier is a highly enthusiastic competitor in this sport and performs with distinction.

The show ring

If you intend to show your puppy, you will need to attend ringcraft classes so you train your dog to perform in the ring and you can also learn about show ring etiquette

When your Border has learnt how to behave in the ring, you are ready to compete. The first classes are for puppies from six months of age and progress through different categories. There are different types of shows you can attend from informal fun day events to the all-important Championship shows where Borders compete for prestigious title of Champion.

Showing is great fun, but at the top level it is highly competitive, so you will need to learn the art of winning – and losing – gracefully.

Health care

We are fortunate that the Border Terrier is a healthy dog, with no exaggerations, and with good routine care, a well-balanced diet, and sufficient exercise, most dogs will experience few health problems.

However, it is your responsibility to put a program of preventative health care in place – and this should start from the moment your puppy, or older dog, arrives in his new home.

Vaccinations

Dogs are subject to a number of contagious diseases. In the old days, these were killers, and resulted in heartbreak for many owners. Vaccinations have now been developed, and the occurrence of the major infectious diseases is now very rare. However, this will only remain the case if all pet owners follow a strict policy of vaccinating their dogs.

There are vaccinations available for the following diseases:

Adenovirus: This affects the liver; affected dogs have a classic 'blue eye'.

Distemper: A viral disease which causes chest and gastro-intestinal damage. The brain may also be affected, leading to fits and paralysis.

Parvovirus: Causes severe gastro enteritis, and most commonly affects puppies.

Leptospirosis: This bacterial disease is carried by rats and affects many mammals, including humans. It causes liver and kidney damage.

Rabies: A virus that affects the nervous system and is invariably fatal. The first signs are abnormal behavior when the infected dog may bite another animal or a person. Paralysis and death follow. Vaccination is compulsory in most countries. In the UK, dogs traveling overseas must be vaccinated.

Kennel Cough: There are several strains of Kennel Cough, but they all result in a harsh, dry, cough. This disease is rarely fatal; in fact most dogs make a good recovery within a matter of weeks and show few signs of ill health while they are affected. However, kennel cough is highly infectious among dogs that live together so, for this reason, most boarding kennels will insist that your dog is protected by the vaccine, which is given as nose drops.

Lyme Disease: This is a bacterial disease transmitted by ticks (see page 170). The first signs are limping, but the heart, kidneys and nervous system can also be affected. The ticks that transmit the disease occur in specific regions, such as the north-east states of the USA, some of the southern states, California and the upper Mississippi region. Lyme disease is still rare in the UK so vaccinations are not routinely offered.

Vaccination program

In the UK, vaccinations are routinely given for distemper, adenovirus, leptospirosis and parvo virus. In the USA, the American Animal Hospital Association advises vaccination for core diseases, which they list as: distemper, adenovirus, parvovirus and rabies. The requirement for vaccinating for non-core diseases – leptospriosis, Lyme disease and kennel cough – should be assessed depending on a dog's individual risk and his likely exposure to the disease.

In most cases, a puppy will start his vaccinations at around eight weeks of age, with the second part given a fortnight later. However, this does vary depending on the individual policy of veterinary practices, and the incidence of disease in your area.

You should also talk to your vet about whether to give annual booster vaccinations. This depends on an individual dog's levels of immunity, and how long a particular vaccine remains effective.

Parasites

No matter how well you look after your Border Terrier, you will have to accept that parasites – internal and external – are ever present, and you need to take preventative action.

Internal parasites: As the name suggests, these parasites live inside your dog. Most will find a home in the digestive tract, but there is also a parasite that lives in the heart. If infestation is unchecked, a dog's health will be severely jeopardized, but routine preventative treatment is simple and effective.

External parasites: These parasites live on your dog's body – in his skin and fur, and sometimes in his ears.

Roundworm

This is found in the small intestine, and signs of infestation will be a poor coat, a pot belly, diarrhoea and lethargy. Pregnant mothers should be treated, but it is almost inevitable that parasites will be passed on to the puppies. For this reason, a breeder will start a worming program, which you will need to continue. Ask your vet for advice on treatment, which will need to continue throughout your dog's life.

Tapeworm

Infection occurs when fleas and lice are ingested. The adult worm takes up residence in the small intestine, releasing mobile segments (which contain eggs) which can be seen in a dog's faeces as small rice-like grains. The only other obvious sign of infestation is irritation of the anus. Again, routine preventative treatment is required throughout your Border's life.

Heartworm

This parasite is transmitted by mosquitoes, and so will only occur where these insects thrive. A warm environment is needed for the parasite to develop, so it is more likely to be present in areas with a warm, humid climate. However, it is found in all parts of the USA, although its prevalence does vary. At present, heartworm is rarely seen in the UK.

Heartworms live in the right side of the heart and larvae can grow up to 14 in (35 cm) in length. A dog with heartworm is at severe risk from heart failure, so preventative treatment, as advised by your vet, is essential. Dogs living in the USA should also have regular tests to check for infection.

Lungworm

Lungworm, or *Angiostrongylus vasorum*, is a parasite that lives in the heart and major blood vessels supplying the lungs. It can cause many problems, such as breathing difficulties, excessive bleeding, sickness and diarrhoea, seizures, and can even be fatal. The parasite is carried by slugs and snails (and their trails), and the dog becomes infected when ingesting these, often accidentally when rummaging through undergrowth.

Lungworm is not common, but it is on the increase. Fortunately, it is easily preventable and affected dogs usually make a full recovery if treated early enough. Your vet will be able to advise you on the risks in your area and what form of treatment may be required.

Fleas

A dog may carry dog fleas, cat fleas, and even human fleas. The flea stays on the dog only long enough to have a blood meal and to breed, but its presence will result in itching and scratching. If your dog has an allergy to fleas – which is usually a reaction to the flea's saliva – he will scratch himself until he is raw.

There are numerous ways of dealing with fleas. Spot-on treatment, which should be administered on a routine basis, is easy to use and highly effective on all types of fleas. For this reason it is one of the most popular methods of flea control.

You can also treat your dog with a spray or with insecticidal shampoo. Bear in mind that the whole environment your dog lives in will need to be sprayed, and all other pets living in your home will also need to be treated.

Ticks

These are blood-sucking parasites which are most frequently found in rural area where sheep or deer are present. The main danger is their ability to pass Lyme disease to both dogs and humans.

Lyme disease is prevalent in some areas of the USA, although it is still rare in the UK. Some areas carry more risk than others, so you should assess the degree of risk in your locality under the guidance of your veterinary surgeon.

The treatment you give your dog for fleas generally works for ticks, but you should discuss the best product to use with your vet.

How to remove a tick

If you spot a tick on your dog, do not try to pluck it off as you risk leaving the hard mouth parts embedded in his skin. The best way to remove a tick is to use a fine pair of tweezers or you can buy a tick remover. Grasp the tick head firmly and then pull the tick straight out from the skin. If you are using a tick remover, check the instructions, as some recommend a circular twist when pulling When you have removed the tick, clean the area with mild soap and water.

Ear mites

These parasites live in the outer ear canal. The signs of infestation are a brown, waxy discharge, and your dog will continually shake his head and scratch his ear. If you suspect your Border has ear mites, a visit to the vet will be needed so that medicated ear drops can be prescribed.

Fur mites

These small, white parasites are visible to the naked eye and are often referred to as 'walking dandruff'. They cause a scurfy coat and mild itchiness. However, they are zoonotic – transferable to humans – so prompt treatment with an insecticide prescribed by your vet is essential.

Harvest mites

These are picked up from the undergrowth, and can be seen as a bright orange patch on the webbing between the toes, although this can also be found elsewhere on the body, such as on the ear flaps. Treatment is effective with the appropriate insecticide.

Skin mites

There are two types of parasite that burrow into a dog's skin. Demodex canis is transferred from a mother to her pups while they are feeding. Treatment is with a topical preparation, and sometimes antibiotics are needed.

The other skin mite is sarcoptes scabiei, which causes intense itching and hair loss. It is highly contagious, so all dogs in a household will need to be treated, which involves repeated bathing with a medicated shampoo.

Common ailments

As with all living animals, dogs can be affected by a variety of ailments. Most can be treated effectively after consulting with your vet, who will prescribe appropriate medication and will advise you on how to care for your dog's needs.

Bear in mind that Border Terriers are well known to vets for having a high pain threshold. You need to be aware of this and if your dog seems off color, he might be in a lot of pain. This is a hard one to do, so it is better to be safe rather than sorry, and to consult your vet if you have any concerns.

Here are some of the more common problems that could affect your Border Terrier, with advice on how to deal with them.

Anal glands

These are two small sacs on either side of the anus, which produce a dark-brown secretion that dogs use when they mark their territory. The anal glands should empty every time a dog defecates but, if they become blocked or impacted, a dog will experience increasing discomfort. He may nibble at his rear end, or 'scoot' his bottom along the ground to relieve the irritation.

Treatment involves a trip to the vet, who will empty the glands manually. It is important to do this without delay or infection may occur.

Dental problems

Good dental hygiene will do much to minimize problems with gum infection and tooth decay. If tartar accumulates to the extent that you cannot remove it by brushing, the vet will need to intervene. In a situation such as this, an anaesthetic will need to be administered so the tartar can be removed manually.

Diarrhoea

There are many reasons why a dog has diarrhoea, but most commonly it is the result of scavenging, a sudden change of diet, or an adverse reaction to a particular type of food. The Border Terrier has a tough constitution, but digestive upset caused by scavenging is not unusual.

If your dog is suffering from diarrhoea, it is important that he does not dehydrate, so make sure that fresh drinking water is available. However, drinking too much can increase the diarrhoea, which may be accompanied with vomiting, so limit how much he drinks at any one time.

Feed a bland diet, such as white fish or chicken with boiled rice for a few days. In most cases, your dog's motions will return to normal and you can resume normal feeding, although this should be done gradually.

However, if this fails to work and the diarrhoea persists for more than two days, you should consult you vet. Your dog may have an infection, which needs to be treated with antibiotics, or the diarrhoea may indicate some other problem which needs expert diagnosis.

Ear infections

The Border Terrier's ears drop forward and lie close to the cheek so air cannot circulate as freely as with ears that are erect or semi erect. It is therefore important to keep a close check on them.

A healthy ear is clean with no sign of redness or

inflammation, and no evidence of a waxy brown discharge or a foul odor. If you see your dog scratching his ear, shaking his head, or holding one ear at an odd angle, you will need to consult your vet.

The most likely causes are ear mites (see page 172), an infection, or there may a foreign body, such as a grass seed, trapped in the ear.

Depending on the cause, treatment is with medicated ear drops, possibly containing antibiotics. If a foreign body is suspected, the vet will need to carry out further investigations.

Eye problems

The Border Terrier's eyes do not protrude, as in breeds such as the Pug, so they are not vulnerable to injury.

However, if your Border's eyes look red and sore, he may be suffering from conjunctivitis. This may, or may not be accompanied with a watery or a crusty discharge. Conjunctivitis can be caused by a bacterial or viral infection, it could be the result of an injury, or it could be an adverse reaction to pollen.

You will need to consult your vet for a correct diagnosis, but in the case of an infection, treatment with medicated eye drops is effective.

Conjunctivitis may also be the first sign of more serious eye problems.

Foreign bodies

In the home, puppies – and some older dogs – cannot resist chewing anything that looks interesting. The toys you choose for your dog should be suitably robust to withstand damage, but children's toys can be irresistible.

Some dogs will chew – and swallow – anything from socks, tights, and other items from the laundry basket, to golf balls and stones from the garden. Obviously, these items are indigestible and could cause an obstruction in your dog's intestine, which is potentially lethal.

The signs to look for are vomiting, and a tucked up posture. The dog will often be restless and will look as though he is in pain. In this situation, you must get your dog to the vet without delay as surgery will be needed to remove the obstruction.

The other type of foreign body that may cause problems is grass seed. A grass seed can enter an orifice such as a nostril, down an ear, the gap between the eye and the eyelid, or penetrate the soft skin between the toes. It can also be swallowed.

The introduction of a foreign body induces a variety of symptoms, depending on the point of entry and where it travels to. The signs to look for include head shaking/ear scratching, the eruption of an abscess, sore, inflamed eyes, or a persistent cough. The vet will be able to make a proper diagnosis, and surgery may be required.

Heatstroke

The Border Terrier is a hardy breed but care should be taken on hot days as heatstroke is a potential danger. When the temperature rises, make sure your dog always has access to shady areas, and wait for a cooler part of the day before going for a walk. Be extra careful if you leave your Border Terrier in the car, as the temperature can rise dramatically – even on a cloudy day. Heatstroke can happen very rapidly, and unless you are able lower your dog's temperature, it can be fatal.

If your Border appears to be suffering from heatstroke, lie him flat and try to reduce his core body temperature by wrapping him in cool towels. A dog should not be immersed in cold water as this will cause the blood vessels to constrict, impeding heat dissipation. As soon as he made some recovery, take him to the vet, where cold intravenous fluids can be administered.

Lameness/limping

There are a wide variety of reasons why a dog can go lame, from a simple muscle strain to a fracture, ligament damage, or more complex problems with the joints. It takes an expert to make a correct diagnosis, so if you are concerned about your dog, do not delay in seeking help.

As your Border Terrier becomes elderly, he may suffer from arthritis, which you will see as general stiffness, particularly when he gets up after resting. It will help if you ensure his bed is in a warm, draught-free location, and, if your Border gets wet after exercise, you must dry him thoroughly.

If your elderly Border seems to be in pain, consult your vet who will be able to help with pain relief medication.

Skin problems

If your dog is scratching or nibbling at his skin, the first thing to check for is fleas (see page 170).There are other external parasites which cause itching and hair loss, but you will need a vet to help you find the culprit.

An allergic reaction is another major cause of skin problems. It can be quite an undertaking to find the cause of the allergy, and you will need to follow your vet's advice, which often requires eliminating specific ingredients from the diet, as well as looking at environmental factors.

Inherited
disorders

The Border Terrier does have a few breed-related disorders. It is important to remember that they can affect offspring so breeding from affected dogs should be discouraged.

There are now recognized screening tests to enable breeders to check for affected individuals and hence reduce the prevalence of these diseases within the breed. DNA testing is also more widely available, and as research into the different genetic diseases progresses, more DNA tests are being developed.

Legg-Calve-Perthes Disease (LCPD)

This is a disease found primarily in terrier breeds where there is a lack of blood supply to the head of the femur (part that interacts with the pelvis) resulting in death of the bone cells in that area. The dead bone cells cause damage to the covering cartilage and there is often ensuing inflammation or arthritis. The cause of LCPD is not known but there is thought to be an hereditary component and an increased risk in any disease that reduces blood flow.

Clinical signs are lameness and pain in one or both back legs, usually seen in dogs less than one year old. Diagnosis will involve initial examination by your vet and then X-rays under anaesthetic with treatment varying dependent on degree of damage. Mild disease may be managed with pain relief and rest, whereas severe disease often requires surgery.

Canine Epileptoid Cramping Syndrome (CECS)

Formerly known as Spike's Disease, CECS is seen in Border Terriers starting between two and six years of age. It is characterized by seizure-like symptoms, loss of balance and muscle spasm but without any loss of consciousness. Often there is abdominal tensing with loud intestinal noises, exaggerated stretching and trembling.

Episodes take from a few seconds to 20 minutes, often worsening each time and disease free intervals reduce with each episode.

The cause is unknown but it is thought to have an hereditary component and is generally thought of as a neurological disorder. Often seen in a number of dogs from the same litter,

there is no particular discrimination between males and females. Response to treatment is often poor but a low protein diet may be beneficial.

Investigations are ongoing to find out the cause, and hence aid treatment, of this disease. Any Border Terrier affected should not be bred from and litter mates should be carefully monitored.

Summing up

It may give the pet owner cause for concern to find about health problems that may affect their dog. But acquiring some basic knowledge is an asset as it will allow you to spot signs of trouble at an early stage. Early diagnosis is very often the means to the most effective treatment, and may even save you from spending more if the disease is more progressed.

If you are concerned at any time about your Border's health, do not self diagnose but consult a vet at the earliest opportunity.

The Border Terrier is a tenacious and brave dog with a zest for life that will keep you and your family entertained and, at times, unable to keep a smile off your face! As one of the generally healthier breeds you will be able to enjoy many happy years together with this loyal canine companion.

Useful addresses

Kennel Clubs
Please contact your Kennel Club to obtain contact information about breed clubs in your area.

UK
The Kennel Club (UK)
1 Clarges Street London, W1J 8AB
Telephone: 0870 606 6750
Fax: 0207 518 1058
Web: www.thekennelclub.org.uk

USA
American Kennel Club (AKC)
5580 Centerview Drive, Raleigh, NC 27606.
Telephone: 919 233 9767
Fax: 919 233 3627
Email: info@akc.org
Web: www.akc.org

United Kennel Club (UKC)
100 E Kilgore Rd, Kalamazoo,
MI 49002-5584, USA.
Tel: 269 343 9020
Fax: 269 343 7037
Web:www.ukcdogs.com/

Australia
Australian National Kennel Council (ANKC)
The Australian National Kennel Council is the administrative body for pure breed canine affairs in Australia. It does not, however, deal directly with dog exhibitors, breeders or judges. For information pertaining to breeders, clubs or shows, please contact the relevant State or Territory Body.

International
Fédération Cynologique Internationalé (FCI)
Place Albert 1er, 13, B-6530 Thuin, Belgium.
Tel: +32 71 59.12.38
Fax: +32 71 59.22.29
Web: www.fci.be/

Training and behavior
UK
Association of Pet Dog Trainers
Telephone: 01285 810811
Web: http://www.apdt.co.uk

Canine Behaviour
Association of Pet Behaviour Counsellors
Telephone: 01386 751151
Web: http://www.apbc.org.uk/

USA
Association of Pet Dog Trainers
Tel: 1 800 738 3647
Web: www.apdt.com/

American College of Veterinary Behaviorists
Web: http://dacvb.org/

American Veterinary Society of Animal Behavior
Web: www.avsabonline.org/

Australia
APDT Australia Inc
Web: www.apdt.com.au

For details of regional behaviourists, contact the relevant State or Territory Controlling Body.

Activities
UK
Agility Club
http://www.agilityclub.co.uk/

British Flyball Association
Telephone: 01628 829623
Web: http://www.flyball.org.uk/

USA
North American Dog Agility Council
Web: www.nadac.com/

North American Flyball Association, Inc.
Tel/Fax: 800 318 6312
Web: www.flyball.org/

Australia
Agility Dog Association of Australia
Tel: 0423 138 914
Web: www.adaa.com.au/

NADAC Australia
Web: www.nadacaustralia.com/

Australian Flyball Association
Tel: 0407 337 939
Web: www.flyball.org.au/

International
World Canine Freestyle Organisation
Tel: (718) 332-8336
Web: www.worldcaninefreestyle.org

Health
UK
British Small Animal Veterinary Association
Tel: 01452 726700
Web: http://www.bsava.com/

Royal College of Veterinary Surgeons
Tel: 0207 222 2001
Web: www.rcvs.org.uk

www.dogbooksonline.co.uk/healthcare/

Alternative Veterinary Medicine Centre
Tel: 01367 710324
Web: www.alternativevet.org/

USA
American Veterinary Medical Association
Tel: 800 248 2862
Web: www.avma.org

American College of Veterinary Surgeons
Tel: 301 916 0200
Toll Free: 877 217 2287
Web: www.acvs.org/

Canine Eye Registration Foundation
The Veterinary Medical DataBases
1717 Philo Rd, PO Box 3007,
Urbana, IL 61803-3007
Tel: 217-693-4800
Fax: 217-693-4801
Web: http://www.vmdb.org/cerf.html

Orthopaedic Foundation of Animals
2300 E Nifong Boulevard
Columbia, Missouri, 65201-3806
Tel: 573 442-0418
Fax: 573 875-5073
Web: http://www.offa.org/

American Holistic Veterinary Medical
Association
Tel: 410 569 0795
Web: www.ahvma.org/

Australia
Australian Small Animal Veterinary
Association
Tel: 02 9431 5090
Web: www.asava.com.au

Australian Veterinary Association
Tel: 02 9431 5000
Web: www.ava.com.au

Australian College Veterinary Scientists
Tel: 07 3423 2016
Web: http://acvsc.org.au

Australian Holistic Vets
Web: www.ahv.com.au/